the weird & wonderful surviveries of
SQUID HORSE
THE MOLLUSC DIMENSION

FIRST EDITION

Edited by The Shaven Raven

With Forewords by
Kim Chin and Dominique Duong

Dear reader...

Hello. Many moons ago, I chose the name Squid because I'm a mysterious, magical, shape-shifting being and I draw with INK! ...Physical, digital, emotional, experiential ink.

For most of my life, I've struggled with my mental health, successfully hiding the chaos for decades. During lockdown, things really unravelled (as for many people), but I couldn't explain how I felt. Around 4am, I'd grab whatever paper was at the top of my scrap drawer and start drawing...

For me, each fragment was a journey — a mood boost, a regulating, a time-hopping, mini- surviverie... The stories are like espressos... overlapping concertinas intensely packed with memories, meanings and more stories. At any point, please pause and skip if needed. You're welcome to read in any order that works for you.

I hope this book inspires more people to try drawing comics!

Thanks for reading & stay curious!
The Mollusc Dimension

CONTENTS

CONTENT NOTES

This book explores racism and racial violence, mental health issues and work trauma.
Specific depictions of particular themes are listed below:

Covid racism — pages 1, 26, 34, 36
Dysregulated eating — page 26
Homophobia — pages 20, 50
Hospital scene — page 20
Sexual harassment and sexual violence — pages 29–30, 44
Transphobia — pages 19, 29–30, 50, 53, 66
Traumatic bereavement — pages 41–45
Workplace violence — pages 29–30

Please look after yourself as you read this. You could ask a trusted person to read it first.
There are some mental health resources at the back of the book.

Foreword by Kim Chin

Intersectional portrayal matters. *The Weird and Wonderful Surviveries of Squid Horse* (WWSSH) by The Mollusc Dimension (TMD) is quirky kaleidoscopic comic that invites readers into the multi-hatted, messy, vulnerable bits of working oneself out, as much as the more put together and hopeful parts of living and connecting. Misunderstandings and frustrations between migrant parents and their geographically different-born offspring — looking the same, but inevitably influenced by the surrounding dominant culture — are laced with humorous observations. Boldy eccentric and surreal, TMD is able to process complex scenarios that span decades into one page of artwork.

Catalysed by a global pandemic, in 2020 it felt a collective consciousness had manifested; as the momentum of Black Lives Matter resurfaced, people came together to fight oppression with masks and all. This was followed by the mobilisation of East and Southeast Asian (ESEA) groups emerging to combat the rise of anti-Asian violence fuelled by overrepresentation of ESEA faces in general news stories reporting on COVID-19.

Like many others, the expanded sense of time created space to examine deep rooted dissonance I had not faced until that point. After relocating abroad for over a decade, I found myself locked down with my octogenarian mum who had different ways of coping with stress of the unknown: Mum found peace in faith, I found it through creating art. Additionally, our mother/daughter history was filtered through a recent diagnosis of ADHD, adding context to many misunderstandings, happy highs, and confusing lows.

Through these many life changes, a friend introduced me to the solidarity group ESEA Sisters. ESEA Sisters emerged from an Instagram call-out for ESEA people to rant, cry, and support each other, our mental health, and our loved ones during increased media stereotyping and hostilities. Being active in ESEA Sisters was a refreshing space of belonging and feeling 'enough' as myself. Participation helped me process both the political and personal realisations that I was traversing. It was through community producing with ESEA Sisters that I met The Mollusc Dimension.

Fast forward to where we both are now. WWSSH had me chuckling, sighing, crying, and twitching with relatability, as someone who has been racialised, sexualised, code-switched, and gaslit. The parental ideology of "achieving" happiness through productivity instead of "being" happy as your authentic self reverberates in "Weird Times" and is a punchline in "Relevance". The inspirational "Goats" summed up my inspired appreciation of racialised-queer-activist-writers and peers who guide my decolonial re-education. The moving dad-centric stories of "Finding Dad" and "The Return" and the complexities of transitioning at the same time personal tragedy struck needed moments of pause and a fresh cup of tea. I felt all the feels and want some of these images as motivational posters in my studio.

If you are a non-ESEA and/or heteronormative reader, the humanness and witty vulnerability of this comic is still a gem; I expect you will be inspired to dig deep, and use whatever big or small privileges you have to abolish imbalanced structures of power that firstly impact those on the margins. The work to rebuild a brighter and equitable future takes diligence. Squid Horse shows us that compassion for others in relation to deeply understanding ourselves, (sprinkled with a bit of humour and creativity) will help make this world a better place for all.

KIM CHIN
Artist, Curator and Community Producer, Co-founder of ESEA Unseen

Foreword by Dominique Duong

*T*he *Weird & Wonderful Surviveries of Squid Horse* is an eclectic collection of autobiographical stories verging on the surreal. We explore The Mollusc Dimension's life from childhood to the adult present, and through it, the issues of mental health, queerness and transness, and what it means to grow up as ESEA diaspora.

Like TMD, I am also an ESEA diasporic (Chinese and Vietnamese), queer comic artist, and I've been working in comics for around seven years now — good God, has it been that long?! It's always heartening to read the work of other ESEA artists, and to see the similarities (as well as the differences) in our cultural and social experiences. There was much I related to, from the mental health and racial issues to the struggle not to place all my self-worth in productivity. What stood out to me most, though, were the stories about family.

As diaspora, so much of who you are is shaped not just by the culture you share with your parents, but the inevitable differences between you.

In TMD's story, "Me Too at Work", a particular panel struck me — when TMD talks about exhibiting art of his character "Tiger Grrrl". His mother expresses that she doesn't like the tiger because it's "scary" and TMD begins to try and explain the meaning, only for Horse (another facet of TMD) to pipe up: *"Forget it. She won't understand."*

I've thought that same thing to myself so many times in relation to my parents, because having to explain yourself and to still be met with blank incomprehension is tiring, *exhausting*. The truth is, there are some things about us diaspora kids that our immigrant parents will never be able to understand, a cultural as well as a generational gulf that feels at times impassable.

This book tells the story of TMD, but at the same time, it's more than that. It's a call for understanding and connection to others and within. All those queer, ESEA and POC readers out there who've experienced something similar, those who've struggled with their mental health, with their art, with finding their place in the world, and those who've not, but are perhaps looking to experience something new: *READ THIS BOOK!* Even if you aren't queer and ESEA, there's still plenty to enjoy and relate to in this collection. And I would say it's always good to read outside of what's familiar to you anyway.

Even with the comics featuring heavier subject matter, TMD's unique art style and sense of humour lends a quirky lightness to the stories being told, especially through his various personas, or with the cute, cartoon-like character designs for his parents.

Despite the difficulties, I wouldn't change being diasporic, where I come from, where my parents come from, for anything. For all the cultural misunderstandings and difficulties being within this middle ground brings — with your family, with the society you're born in and yet doesn't always accept you, within yourself — it also brings so much joy, and pride, and you can feel that in this book, too.

DOMINIQUE DUONG

Illustrator and Comic Book Artist

character guide

Name: Joonkid 馬俊傑

About: The author's present incarnation. I wear a beanie hat & small hoop earrings.

Feels: Sleepy...

Likes: Ice cream, baking, absurdi-tea!

Dislikes: KUMQUATS

Name: Squid (he/him)

About: Oooh... when do you need this back? I wear a stripey t-shirt.

Feels: Uh...I don't know... maybe anxious?

Likes: Trees ♡ the sea

Dislikes: Surprises. Wet sleeves.

Name: HORSE

About: WHAT IS THE ACTUAL POINT OF THIS QUESTION?!/ MY VIBE IS SUMMER GOTH-PUNK-JAZZ.

Feels: CANTANKEROUS!!!!! WORLD-I'M OUT TO GET YOU!...ALSO EXHAUSTED COS ADHD.

Likes: WORK, GRUMBLING, SMALLTALK,

Dislikes: DOGS, BIGOTS

Name: coolhead mollusc

About: i'm a songwriter & composer! i wear a black hat, white shirt, black tie & vintage pointy shooos.

Feels: kitsch & wanderful

Likes: when folks singalong ♫

Dislikes: dodgy keyboard stands

Name: Squid Mum

About: I am? an OWL!

Feels: VERY BUSY

Likes: presents! Dogs. Music.

Dislikes: lateness, surprises,

Name: Dad

About: Late father of the author — sun sign Leo.

Feels: Adventurous!

Likes: Baking, opera

Dislikes: I loathe crowds!

Name: THE SUN

About: MAGNETIC, GENDERFLUID HOT BALL OF PLASMA. MY PHD WAS ON "DIVINING DRAG — DUST, STEAM AND MAGNETIC MOUSTACHES".

Feels: HELD TOGETHER BY MY OWN GRAVITY.

Likes: BEING ORBITED

Dislikes: PAPARAZZI. TCH! THIS PHOTO!

Name: Younger Squid/s

About: We are Squid aged 2 years to late 20s. We're usually but not always in a stripey t-shirt.

Feels: Stuff.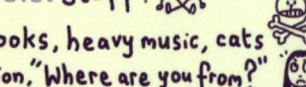

Likes: Drawing, books, heavy music, cats

Dislikes: the question, "Where are you from?"

FOR MORE CHARACTER CARDS, JUMP TO PAGE 70

weird times

Deadline – Work – Lockdown – Therapy
In this house I feel – Sadness –Another day – Notes

deadline

work

lockdown

therapy

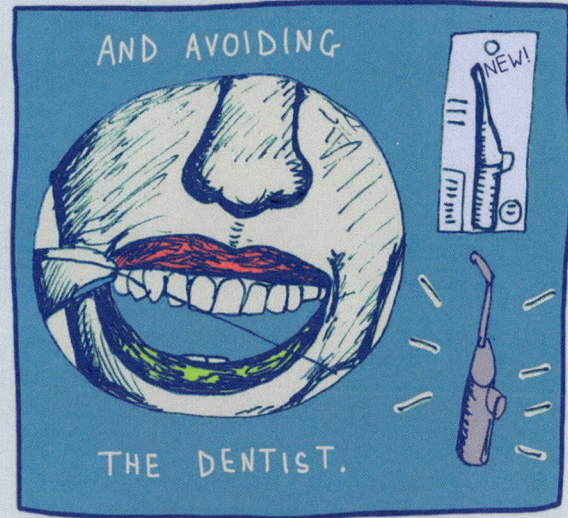

another day

notes on *weird times*

For readers who'd like some more context...
Or feel free to skip and move on to the next set of stories!
Or feel free to take a break!

WORK + BEING ESEA + NEURODIVERGENT

As a British-born East Asian, WORK was how I hid my feelings and struggles. *If I got A's in school, no one would notice I was struggling.* People have opened up to me about workaholism and/or hiding emotional pain through work. I sense that the children of immigrants are prone to this, but it could happen to anyone. After discovering I have ADHD, a lot of things have started to make sense and I wish more ESEA parents would embrace, explore and support neurodivergence in their children and possibly in themselves.

TIME-TRAVELLING

Squid, Horse and Coolhead Mollusc represent different sides of me during lockdown (anxiety, depression and creativity) but gradually they started to overlap and appear in stories from my past experiences including childhood.

THERAPY

Unaware of the impact of the pandemic, I had chosen to quit therapy around the start of 2020! Quite simply, the worst timing. So I was without a therapist until the late Spring of 2021. Creativity was a lifeline for me. As an adult, I continue to cope with difficult emotions through art. After much searching, I found my current therapist and it makes so much difference reflecting on things with someone who is both queer and ESEA!

REST

I find it hard to relax and this is connected to workaholism. Among QTIBIPOC and/or disabled friends, reclaiming resting and napping is radical. Due to ADHD and anxiety, I don't sleep well. Having a nap helps me to recharge before working in the afternoon. Maybe, this is not such a strange idea... in some cultures, it's quite usual to have a rest in the afternoon. Like many artists, sleeping and dreaming are states I love exploring in art because anything can happen!

growing pains &
awkward times

Imagination — Racism — Art teachers
Awkward times — '80s kid, '90s teen
How I survived my teenage years — University

awkward times

HOW I SURVIVED MY TEENAGE YEARS

1. Finally got my ears pierced – on a school geography trip.

2. Wished and wondered

3. Won the school cake contest with my entry, "The Poltergeist"

4. Lost myself in books & art

5. Got the 6-year old staying with my family into Nirvana

6. Practised piano for hours

7. Swore — but only secretly

8. Spent ages trying to dye my hair even though

9. Bought stuff I needed

10. Went to live music gigs

11. Met my future self

12. Daydreamt about my girlfriend at work

13. Watched the sunrise in Scarborough

guilt & goats

relevance

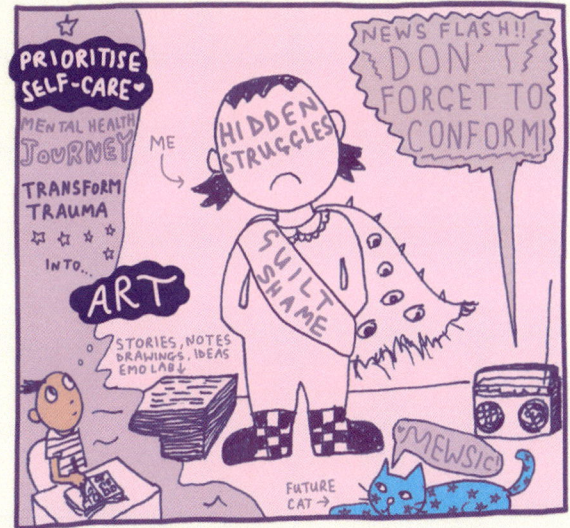

One summer in my teens, I was doing work experience for a charity.

ME (Lunch!)

I was out on my lunch break. One moment, loads of other people were there.

Suddenly, I felt a hand on my body! The next moment, I heard myself bellowing at the horrible man.

LEAVE ME ALONE!

I was so loud, people across the road looked over.

Seeming to wither at my rage, he slunk away.

When I got back to the office, one of the staff asked why I was crying.

Maybe it's a good idea to go home early today.

Everyone was kind to me.

I can't remember if I told my parents at the time — or at all...? In 2001 I drew "Tiger Grrrl" which I exhibited at a small art show. She appeared on posters, t-shirts, stickers and an anti-Trump protest. But Mum said:

I DON'T LIKE THE TIGER. IT'S SCARY!

It's about...

FORGET IT. SHE WON'T UNDERSTAND.

I decided to join a "Reclaim the Night" March with my then partner. We were both very anxious! Back then, I identified as a trans man. I'd heard a queer, cis woman I admired say men shouldn't be part of the "metoo" movement.

MY BODY!

RESPECT ALL WOMEN

decolonise feminism

TRANS PRIDE

I WISH I'D APPROACHED HER FOR A CHAT.

I THOUGHT OF WHAT SHE SAID AND I SILENCED MYSELF.

UNTIL NOW. WITH THIS STORY.

SOMETIMES I WISH I'D SHARED WHILE I IDENTIFIED AS A WOMAN.

I WANTED TO WRITE THIS BOOK TO REACH... ♥ PEOPLE ♥

From my teens to my late 20s, I worked about 9 customer service jobs.

Nearly all my bosses were white men and most of them were fine, but there was this ONE VIOLENT CREEP.

I THINK IT WAS THE LAST TIME I WORKED IN A BAR.

I should have known at the interview. #offvibes

ME THEN →

I'm living at home but I want to buy stuff, food, go on holiday...

HIS WIFE WAS SOUTHEAST ASIAN. SHE WAS REALLY NICE BUT HE WAS A NASTY PIECE OF WORK.

One evening, I'd just worked a bank holiday thinking it would be double pay. He paid me cash-the usual rate, so I queried this - politely.

HE WAS SO IRATE, HE TRIED TO CHOKE ME AND HISSED, "YOU'RE ALL ABOUT THE MONEY AREN'T YOU!"

Of course I was about the money. It was a job! I was working for money!

Then there was this "friend" who helped me with animation and tech stuff.

One day, he said he'd helped me a lot but wasn't getting anything in return. I realised my error and offered to draw him some illustrations or an animation. I was confused by his response.

I WANT A MASSAGE.

ME ↓

Oh dear! Maybe I could BOOK him a massage??!

My accidental revenge on the pub landlord.

I was at band practice when he called me. As it was noisy, I misheard him say he was going on holiday, so I said (very cheerfully),

have a nice holiday!!

Turns out, he was going to his cousin's funeral.

OOPS.

IT WAS TIME TO QUIT THAT JOB... FOREVER

ME IN A BAND

WHEN I FIRST CAME OUT AS TRANS TO MY FAMILY, THEY WERE OPPOSED TO THE IDEA AND ALSO DISAPPOINTED!

They said, "Our family has strong women!"

♫ Why do family, friends & strangers tell us we're not asian enough... ♫

Creating comics, zines, music and poetry has really helped my mental health and also helped people to better understand me.

directions

guilt

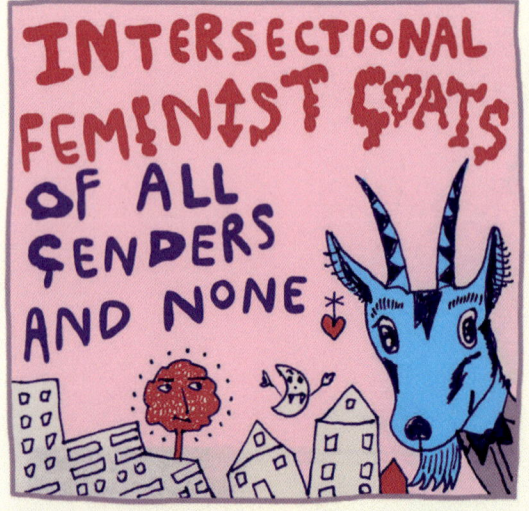

notes on *guilt & goats*

As before... feel free to skip this and move on to the next set of stories!
Or feel free to take a break!

SURVIVERIES

Several years ago, I was astonished to read artist Jet Moon's definition of "survivor", which included discrimination, e.g. racism and homophobia. It was the first time I felt I could identify as a survivor. Since then, I realised that some of my experiences could be defined as sexual violence and violence. I made up the word "surviveries" — an amalgamation of the words "survive","convivial" (co-exist) and "jardinerie" (French for garden centre). It's pronounced "sir-vy-veries" (where "vy" rhymes with "bye").

CORONARACISM

A term combining "corona" (from coronavirus) + "racism". Since 2020, many ESEA were globally subjected to hostile and/or violent behaviour from non-Asians.

THE TREE OF KNOWLEDGE

Taking place in lockdown, this story refers ironically to "'80s child, '90s teen". In the Old Testament, the Tree of Knowledge story bears forbidden fruit, which represents transgression/rebellion. Squid, Horse and Coolhead Mollusc stealing the bread represents how trans people and our allies unite to resist and dismantle transphobia.

Today's terfiarchy (another vocabulary invention from me — you're welcome!) descends from the archaic (hence "Dodo" the fictional Twitter tag) *tradition of toxic cis women serving the patriarchy.* As a survivor of traumas, I am beginning to explore my vulnerabilty in healthful ways and to understand the influence of colonialism on my thinking (and my traumas). Oh and I've been baking sourdough bread since August 2023!

SPOON THEORY

"A metaphor describing the amount of physical or mental energy that a person has available for daily activities and tasks, and how it can become limited. The term was coined in a 2003 essay by American writer Christine Miserandino." (Wikipedia).

hall of fame

— folks & journeys

the mumness

day out

glasses

dad's stories

finding dad — an operetta

FINDING DAD

A SUMMER TRAGEDY

IT WAS AN ORDINARY FRIDAY EVENING.

MY PARENTS WERE ON HOLIDAY.

I WAS ABOUT TO GO TO BED

WHEN MUM TEXTED: YOUR DAD IS MISSING!!

THE NEXT DAY, MY FRIEND ME BOOK MY FLIGHT.

IN THE TAXI I WROTE A SONG ABOUT LOOKING FOR DAD. I WAS ANXIOUS AS I'D ONCE HEARD SINÉAD O'CONNOR SAY HER SONG LYRICS BECAME TRUE!

AT THE AIRPORT, THE LUGGAGE CHECK MAN MADE A SEXIST JOKE.

AT LEAST WE DIDN'T ASK YOU TO TAKE OFF YOUR BRA. HA HA HA.

THAT WAS INAPPROPRIATE! COMPLAINTS

I need TEA BAGS!

Hi! DUTY FREE! TEA

What are you doing here?

I've come to help you find Uncle.

MY COUSIN AND I FLEW TO JOIN SQUIDMUM.

CAN YOU BELIEVE IT? MY COUSIN WAS THE ONLY ONE OF US WITH A SMARTPHONE.

SQUID! You'll be on TV in 5 minutes.

It's Squid! He's on the news! MEWS

Please help us spread the word and find him!

THE HOTEL STAFF KEPT BRINGING US FRUIT PLATTERS

WELL-MEANING PEOPLE KEPT SUGGESTING UNFAMILIAR AND CREEPY RITUALS

We were desperate

WHERE WAS DAD?!! HE'D TOTALLY VANISHED!!!

HAD DAD BEEN DAD-NAPPED?

BY ALIENS!

44

MY FRIEND FLEW IN TO HELP US FIND DAD.

MOUNTAIN RESCUE SEARCHED TIRELESSLY.

Sorry. Nothing yet.

MORE FRUIT KEPT ARRIVING.

EVERYTHING WAS BEAUTIFUL BUT WE HAD NO APPETITE.

THE POLICE COULDN'T FIND ANYTHING.

?!?? ? ?!?

MY FLATMATE TEXTED ME THE EXAM RESULTS FOR MY PIANO DIPLOMA.

I got distinction?!

Oh... Who cares?!

THEN, LATE ONE NIGHT...

KNOCK KNOCK!

HE'S BEEN FOUND.

THEY'D BEEN LOOKING ON THE WRONG MOUNTAIN!

IT WAS A SPLENDID VIEW HE FELL FOR.

MUM REMEMBERED A FRIENDLY LOCAL WHO'D LENT US HER KETTLE.

If there's anything else you need...

?? ? ?

We're really not supposed to be here...

WE PERSUADED HER TO DRIVE US TO THE PLACE WHERE HE DIED.

THE RETURN

WHEN WE CAME BACK, MUM WAS AFRAID OF TREES.

please pull the blind.

SHE BECAME OBSESSED WITH FINDING DAD'S PHONE.

Can you email the lawyer again?

I did! Three times...

A BUNCH OF THINGS HAPPENED

THE ROOF IS LEAKING!

WE MOVED THE PIANO.

THEN I MOPPED THE ROOF.

One day, I heard a strange noise.

@#!*

THE BATHROOM'S FLOODED!!!

Thank you so much!

LUCKILY OUR NEIGHBOUR HELPED US. BUT THEN

The ceiling fell down right next to me!!

AS DAD TOOK PRIDE IN DEALING WITH MOST OF THE BILLS, WE HAD A SLIGHT PROBLEM...

WE DIDN'T KNOW WHO MUM'S SERVICES WERE WITH!

RING RING!

Hiii. It's time to renew your insurance!

I am SO glad you called! Now I know who mum has insurance with!

DAD PREFERRED TO RUN THE SHOW.

Maybe he couldn't delegate. Did he have issues with control?

Also... he left no will.

I guess it wasn't the ideal time to socially transition.

SHE/HER → HE/HIM

BUT I'D WAITED LONG ENOUGH!

uugh... ANOTHER LETTER FOR DAD

Yeah. Could you delete him from your mail list please?

Something had been going on for me BEFORE Dad went missing!

WHEN I CAME OUT AS TRANS, I WOKE UP WRAPPED IN A HUGE TRANS FLAG AND EVERYONE GAVE ME FREE TRANS CAKE!

Wait a minute! THAT IS NOT HOW IT HAPPENED!

STRETCH

FIRST, I MADE A— TIRAMISU (WITH CATS)

THEN I TRIED SOME VEGAN SUSHI

MY DAD GAVE US A RIDE TO A GIG

DAD VANISHED AND MUM FOUND THE CHANGE HARD.

MY PRONOUNS ARE HE/HIM

I PERFORMED IN LGBTIQA+ SPACES ♥

WRITING SONGS HELPED ME THROUGH LONELINESS AND TO FIND FRIENDSHIP, AND LOVE!

MY GP REFUSED TO REFER ME TO THE GENDER CLINIC—TIL I TOOK A TRANS GUY ON T TO MEET HER.

Hi! OK.

DOCTOR'S JAW →

DREW LOTS OF MR. CARROT COMICS

You'll be ok...

TOP SURGERY GLOW

2018

ESEA COMMUNITY WALK ♥

2024

HERE WE ARE... OUTSIDE... TOGETHER

O-O

Dating

This HAS to end!!

BUT WHY?!

But we're in love and we just want a weekend away...

And she said

WELL... I GUESS YOU'RE GOING FAR AWAY TO UNIVERSITY ANYWAY...

I was a MISERABLE fresher.

I do rant quite a bit about the cishet men I dated... but...

One boyfriend helped me EMBROIDER a banner ALL NIGHT for a fundraiser! POMPOMS CHARITY SHOP SATIN

Then my heart was stolen by another! ISN'T GREECE BEAUTIFUL? There are so many cats!

Then my girlfriend LOVED my disco ball!

Then a brief thing that didn't work out and involved a HEFTY train fine!

Then a significant but toxic relationship. ← 28 LILIES

He knew I didn't like them, but he LOVED them. An odd "take-me-back" gift...!!

I dated another artist. We went on a screenprint date. MINE WENT WRONG

I was jealous and insecure and had this FEELING his mum hated me on sight. SORRY... I HAVE TO GO TO WORK NOW... SEE YOU AROUND...

Then I had a crush on a poor, unsuspecting bookseller!

When I dated a guy who was lead singer in a band, I wondered What's it like being in a BAND?

Alas, again my heart was stolen by another...! I WANT TO EXPERIENCE THE NORTHERN LIGHTS WITH YOU. Uhh... Too cold!!

He got a job (in Hong Kong!) and I was jealous and insecure (again!) BYE.

I went on a first date and I was so bored... we ended up seeing each other for a few weeks! SO BORED!

After more searching, I nearly went on a date with another lead singer guy...And FINALLY I REALIZED...

cloud bear

in search of wonder (re)finding joy

Birthday parties — Three things — Lonely piano
Singing teachers — Take me back to the ocean
Asians have feelings too

birthday parties

BIRTHDAY PARTIES

AT MY 2ND BIRTHDAY PARTY, FOR FUN, SOMEONE PUT A PLATE ON MY HEAD!

(AND I'VE BEEN A SURREALIST EVER SINCE...)

ONCE, MY MUM MADE ME WEAR A HIDEOUS DRESS!

THE BIRTHDAY GIRL'S DAD WALKED IN THROUGH THE BACK DOOR...

NICE DRESS!! ACTUALLY DID NO ONE MENTION THAT I NEED YOU TO HELP ME WITH THE GARDENING?

I WAS HORRIFIED! I DIDN'T KNOW HE WAS JOKING...

BUT IT GOT WORSE!

WE ALL GOT TO HOLD THE PET HAMSTER, BUT WHEN IT WAS MY GO, SHE ESCAPED!

IF I TELL THEM I FOUND YOU, I GET AN EXTRA PIECE OF CAKE!

TWO MINUTES, I'VE NEARLY FINISHED MY BOOK!

MUM WOULDN'T LET ME GO TO A "CATS, THE MUSICAL" PARTY. SHE SAID IT WASN'T "PROPER MUSIC". BUT LUCKILY, SHE WAS OK WITH THE

PIRATE PARTY!

CHECK OUT MY FIRST DRAWN-ON MOUSTACHE AND STIFF "BUTCH" STANCE. SOOO QUEER!

IN MY LATE TWENTIES AND EARLY THIRTIES, I LOVED HOSTING PARTIES AT MY EAST LONDON FLAT-SHARE. I ENDED UP MOVING BACK HOME—MUCH FURTHER FOR MY FRIENDS, YET THEY STILL CAME...

HERE THEY ARE RUNNING FOR THE TUBE HOME ON A SUNDAY EVENING, AFTER MY BIRTHDAY KALEIDOSCOPE-MAKING QUASI-BACCHANAL!

ON MY 42ND BIRTHDAY, I WENT TO KEW GARDENS WITH FRIENDS. THE JOURNEY AND PLANNING TOOK AAAAGES... BUT IT WAS WORTH IT.

IT'S SO MAGICAL!

three things

SOMETIMES I DON'T KNOW WHERE I'M GOING...

AND IN THE STRANGEST OF PLACES...

I STUMBLE

UPON REMNANTS

OF MYSELF.

WITH MUSIC... EVEN LONELINESS FEELS COLOURFUL.

THE VOID HAS RHYTHM...

I SING MY FEARS

singing teachers

Random question... Want to hear some songs?

Take me back to the ocean
Asians have feelings too
Place like now

Oh and... do you *hate* getting to the end of
a book you're enjoying? I do...

You're coming to the end of the stories...
Turn the page to read the last story!

♫ SOMETIMES I WANNA BE A WHITE QUEER LIVING IN BRIGHTON

OH YEAH!

SOMETIMES I WANNA BE AN ASIAFILE TOO!

AGGRESSIVE NIHAO!

I spent my gap year in... (PROCEEDS TO LIST 2-3 EAST/SOUTHEAST ASIAN COUNTRIES)

Are you Chinese or Japanese?

I'm from Essex!

(ANOTHER!) AGGRESSIVE NIHAO *

Chinese children are so cute!

All my exes are Asian!

But ALL children are cute!

Or maybe that's patronising!

just squidding!

i don't really want to be an asiaphile!

There are days when I feel left on the shelf...

WHY CAN'T I JUST BE MYSELF??

Aw. That's MY LAST story — for now!

THANK YOU for reading "The Weird & Wonderful Surviveries of Squid Horse".

(Keep going for some EXTRA CONTENT!)

WWSSH TRIVIA

WHILE EDITING THIS BOOK I...*

BAKED...
44 sourdough loaves
34 sourdough pizzas
182 sourdough muffins

DRANK...
4237 cups of decaf breakfast tea

NAPPED
320 times

WALKED SQUIDMUM'S DOG

406 times

RE-LETTERED EACH STORY
6+ times

From scanning the **FIRST** drawing to printing,** it took
1411 DAYS! That's...
3 YEARS, 10 MONTHS, 2 WEEKS & 2 DAYS

* Since August 2023
** Since August 2020

character guide continued

Name: Polly
About: SquidMum's emotional support harrier beagle.

Feels: HUNGRY-always
Likes: Food! Walks! Bum scratches!
Dislikes: Foxes, squirrels, holidays :((

Name: tea
About: delicious aromatic beverage

Feels: refreshing
Likes: hot water
Dislikes: being forgotten :(

Name: ALICE
About: LIVED WITH SQUID + FAMILY SINCE I WAS A TINY KITTEN. WINNER OF BEST CAT AWARD.

Feels: VERY SOFT
Likes: DRIED CUTTLEFISH, SQUID'S BED
Dislikes: FLUTE MUSIC

Name: Cloud Bear
About: aka Cumulus ursus. Writer. Studied Linguistics, then Creative Writing. Moved from Brighton to live with Squid and 'the Whirlwind'.

Feels: fizzy
Likes: Books, animals, clouds, Queen (the band!!)
Dislikes: Mushrooms

Name: REAPER
About: MYSTERIOUS DRIVER (EX-SAILING CHAMPION). FULLY BOOKED FOREVER. AGELESS.

Feels: OK-LA...AND YOU?
Likes: ?
Dislikes: TRAFFIC WARDENS

Name: A tree. One of many!
About: Home for creatures. Celebri-tree with deep roots. Air to the thrown ☆

Feels: More humans could hug me.
Likes: growing
Dislikes: borders, climate change >:((

Name: Guan Yin. Actually I have many names!
About: Awakening traveller. Beyond gender.

Feels: Floaty
Likes: Compassion
Dislikes: genocide, elitism, transphobia

Name: BLU
About: TRANS-MASC LEGEND

Feels: MAGICAL
Likes: FLYING. SWIMMING IS OK TOO.
Dislikes: BOXES. BORDERS

THERE ARE MORE CHARACTER CARDS ON PAGE 5!

Name: Piano AKA Pianoforte

About: I make beautiful music when my keys are DEPRESSED!!

Feels: Dramatic. Sensitive. Kind.

Likes: Musicians. Your secrets.

Dislikes: RAIN. ERASER SHAVINGS!

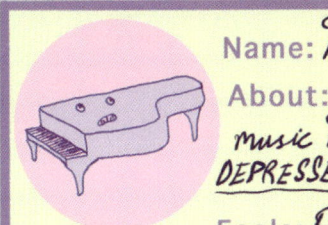

Name: KEILEON (QUILIN)

About: LEGENDARY TRANS ASIAN UNICORN. QI MEANS "MASCULINE" & "LIN" MEANS "FEMININE".

Feels: LUCKY

Likes: INTEGRITY. CHIPS

Dislikes: RUNNING OUT OF KETCHUP

Name: ALIENS

About: DAD-STEALING, CAKE-OPERA FIENDS

Feels: PECKISH. SOUR.

Likes: CHERRY CLAFOUTIS

Dislikes: MARBLE CAKE-IT'S TOO DRY!

Name: 3

About: Book-loving friend of Squid.

Feels: kind. sarcastic. playful

Likes: chocolate. purple. East coast hiphop

Dislikes: harpsichord. financial admin

Name: Great white Terf (aka toxic femininity)

About: The Patriarchy's best kept secret.

Feels: like white saviourism

Likes: ignoring pre-colonial trans history

Dislikes: Being labelled a terf. Trans activists.

Name: CLOUD

About: AN INTERNATIONAL OR!!! MIGHT-I-SAY... UNIVERSAL SENSATION!

Feels: TRANSFORMATIVE.

Likes: PEOPLE-WATCHING. SHAPE-SHIFTING

Dislikes: WIND DURING YOGA.

READER! I INVITE YOU TO IMAGINE FILLING IN THIS CARD!

Name: FRIENDZ 'N' OTHER MAGICAL BEINGZ

About: THOUGHTFUL, ART-LOVING, MUSIC-INHALING, BOOK-GUZZLING, QUIRKY INTROVERT.

Feels: OPEN-MINDED

Likes: OXYGEN, WATER & COOLHEAD'S MUSIC!

Dislikes: ABLEISM

Name:

About:

Feels:

Likes:

Dislikes:

mental health resources

If you need to talk to someone about any topics covered in this book (or anything else), here are some UK helplines:

befrienders.org

childline.org.uk — Here to help anyone under 19 in the UK with any issue they're going through.

giveusashout.org — UK's first and only free, confidential, 24/7 text messaging service.

mermaidsuk.org.uk — Supports trans, non binary and gender-questioning children & young people.

mind.org.uk

samaritans.org

switchboard.lgbt

If you're outside the UK:

findahelpline.com

helpguide.org/find-help.htm

THROUGH THESE, YOU MAY BE ABLE TO DISCOVER MANY MORE ESEA RESOURCES & PRACTITIONERS.

ESEA RESOURCES

BESEA.N (British East and Southeast Asian Network) — A community focused, volunteer-led organisation with a mission to empower, educate and embrace East and South East Asian people — and their allies! — in the UK. **besean.co.uk**

ESEA Heritage Month — A collaborative programme of events, dedicated to East and South East Asian heritage, culture, history and everything in between. Founded by BESEA.N. **eseaheritagemonth.co.uk**

ESEA SISTERS — Spaces for East and South East Asian women, trans, non-binary and genderqueer folk to share joy and resistance. **linktr.ee/EseaSisters**

ON YOUR SIDE — A hate crime and hate incidents report and support service for East and Southeast Asians based in the UK. **onyoursideuk.org**

SEEAC (Southeast and East Asian Centre) — A community organisation for and by migrants, refugees and people seeking asylum from Southeast and East Asia and people of these heritages living in the UK. **seeac.org.uk**

bookclub /reflective questions

1. Horse avoids talking about emotions by working. Do you find this relatable? Or not? How might you encourage Horse to open up?

2. Does the behaviour of any of the characters remind you of anyone you know?

3. Squid, Horse and Coolhead Mollusc represent different sides of the author in co-existence. What contrasting sides of yourself are there? Do they ever meet in conversation?

4. At various points, the characters enjoy being in nature with the trees or the sea. Do you have any positive memories or recent experiences spending time outdoors or leisure time?

5. Food preparation, sharing and gifts are one of the "languages" referred to in the book. Do you have experiences regarding food as communication you'd like to share?

6. Which story or stories spoke to you the most? Were there any that felt confusing? Or felt difficult?

7. The colour palettes for "Imagination", "Dad's Stories" and "Asians Have Feelings Too" refer to Chinese ceramics. Which colour palettes are your favourite? Why?

8. Are there some themes or ideas in the book which might inspire you to create a mini-comic?

9. Feel free to create your own questions and discuss topics. If you can't access a bookclub, maybe you could form your own bookclub with a friend or two!

List of stories

HALL OF FAME — FOLKS & JOURNEYS

IN SEARCH OF WONDER — (RE)FINDING JOY

a little extra sleep

THANK YOU!

Enormous thanks to my WWSSH team for believing this project — my book editor, The Shaven Raven, for her dedication, professionalism and patience on our 1st book and nth project! To my foreword writers, Kim Chin and Dominique Duong for diving deep into my stories and sharing their own. To my mentor Rachael House for her generosity and invaluable insights. My continuity advisor, Boe Studios for improving the flow. My proofreader, Dr. Puck Fletcher, and sensitivity reader, Eris Young for their attention to detail and warmth.

Thank you to all the inspirational artists, writers and speakers I consulted on my journey: Amy Phung, Eris Young, Dr. Jamie Pei, Len Lukowski, Lishan Chan, Maisie Chan, MG Zimeta and Peter Collins. To Amy Phung, Dr. Diana Yeh and Fox Fisher for the thoughtful, appreciative words. To Lydia Stockbridge and Christy Ku (access workers) and Suyin Haynes — thank you for advising me. Thank you to LDComics, Rona Luo, JK Mak, Tanka Studios, The Common Press and Gosh Comics (London), The Bookish Type (Leeds) and The Queery (Brighton) for supporting my publishing journey.

"Coronaracism" was first published on the BESEA.N blog: "From the shame of coronaracism to queer confidence" (September 2021). Thank you to BESEA.N for letting me share my raw story back then, platforming my work, which crucially helped me to start connecting with ESEA people and for all your work for ESEA and our allies. Thank you to ESEA Sisters, SEEAC, Kanglungan and all ESEA community endeavours for your commitment, vision, welcoming events and the most delicious snacks!

Enormous appreciation to ALL my friends and supporters for your encouragement and enthusiasm! To Ash L, Fimi and Maggs Dao for your contribution towards my AHFT song comic. To SquidMum and P2 (aka SquidCuz) for assuring me my Chinese characters are sort of readable, and to my family for being interested in and supporting my work. Thanks to Alexis Deacon, Claudia Matosa, my comics study group, Dafydd Palfrey, Eva Megias, Franki Ayres, Kitsune Art, Lana Lê, Ludo Foster, MG Zimeta, Mike Armstrong, Dr. Nicola Streeten, Nick Bryant, RayCanDoArt, Tom W, Uwu Wizard, Wallis Eates, WIP Comics and Yen Godden for your support and chats. Thank you accessible LGBTIQA+ spaces. Tentacle waves to everyone who's received a frantic midnight email (or 6) from me.

Thank you to London Writers' Salon, where I wrote my funding apps and developed and edited the book for a squillion hours. Thanks to LiLy K Bright for telling me about LWS, Everyday Writes and many helpful neurodivergent resources. Thank you to Tara (Shaded Writers/Open Minds Project) for the fruitful Sunday QTIBIPOC poetry workshops and The Grange Projects for a dreamy residency.

I am very grateful that this book was created using public funding by the National Lottery through Arts Council England.

Thank you to EVERYONE for supporting me by reading, buying, borrowing, sharing about this book and/or my zines and sharing on social media. Your efforts, interest and solidarity mean so much!

Panel 6, "Awkward Times" was first published in queer and neurodivergent—friendly magazine, *Snowflake Magazine*, The Heritage Issue (2024).

DISCLAIMER: This is a demi—autobiographical work as recalled by the author, with elements of fantasy. For privacy reasons, names have been changed or omitted. The viewpoints expressed are the author's own.

TITLE: The Weird & Wonderful Surviveries of Squid Horse

ISBN: 978-1-80517-723-4
AUTHOR: The Mollusc Dimension
BOOK MEDIA FORMAT: Paperback
DESCRIPTION: First paperback edition

MAIN DESCRIPTION: For as long as he can remember, Squid has drawn comics to process anxiety and confusion, and since his teens, Horse's friends and family have been puzzled by his depressive rages. After cataclysmic events, Squid and Horse go on a fragmented adventure with dream—like twists, encountering weird memories, past and present selves and magical discoveries! You're invited to dip or dive into this quirky debut autobiographical collection of 37 self—contained yet interwoven short comic stories. Based on the unique (yet relatable) lived experiences of The Mollusc Dimension, a British—born Chinese, queer, trans, neurodivergent artist, this book is about surviving multiple hidden challenges and daring to imagine.

SUBJECTS: Graphic novels/comic books.
Coming out — Graphic non—fiction. | Grief — Graphic non—fiction. | Identity — Graphic non—fiction. |

KEYWORDS: ADHD, Anxiety, Artist, Asian, Autobiography, Bereavement, British Asian, British—Chinese, Chinese, Coming out, Community, Creativity, Depression, ESEA, East and Southeast Asian, Family, Gender, Grief, Growing up, Intersectional, LGBT, LGBTIQA, Mental health, Neurodivergence, Non binary, Queer, Racism, Trans, Transgender

AUDIENCE: Ages 14 and up

Publication Date: October 2024
Page Count: 80
(Chiefly) Illustrations: (colour)
Spine size: 9mm
Trim size: 18 cm x 25 cm
Weight: 330g

Designed and printed in the UK